YOU KNOW YOU'RE A **CHILD** OF THE

80s

WHEN...

Mark Leigh and
Mike Lepine

summersdale

YOU KNOW YOU'RE A CHILD OF THE 80s WHEN...

First published in 2004, reprinted 2006 and 2009
This revised edition copyright © Summersdale Publishers Ltd, 2011
Icons © Shutterstock

Summersdale Publishers Ltd
46 West Street
Chichester
West Sussex
PO19 1RP
UK

www.summersdale.com

Printed and bound in China

ISBN: 978-1-84953-163-4

Substantial discounts on bulk quantities of Summersdale books are available to corporations, professional associations and other organisations. For details contact Summersdale Publishers by telephone: +44 (0) 1243 771107, fax: +44 (0) 1243 786300 or email: nicky@summersdale.com.

To....................................

From................................

You know you're a child of the 80s when...

Your party piece is doing the Rubik's Cube in less than 40 seconds. That or reciting all the words to 'Vienna'.

You thought Simon Le Bon and the other Duran Duran lads were the finest male specimens you'd ever seen, even though they wore lipstick, blusher and big girls' blouses.

You remember being a bit suspicious of microwave food – you thought it might be radioactive.

You wore neon socks – odd ones too – thinking they made you look 'street'.

You believed your older brother when he told you that Phil Oakey could only afford half a haircut on his pop star salary.

You did all your school essays on paper with a fountain pen and you would go to the library to do all your research.

You don't remember gap years – people who didn't go straight to uni were just doing resits.

You used to wake up to
Mad Lizzie, Rustie Lee,
Wincey Willis and
Golden Grahams.

You were gutted that
Prince Charles got married,
but decided to hold out for
Edward instead.

You graffitied a CND symbol on your school satchel along with lyrics to The Smiths' 'There is a Light that Never Goes Out'.

You religiously bought every issue of *Smash Hits* and would test your friends at lunchtimes on the song lyrics printed in the middle pages.

Your Filofax was full of
practice signatures for
your future life as
Mrs Adam Ant.

You remember Paul McCartney best for being in Wings.

If you didn't have a long shaggy perm, you were a social outcast. Same for your partner.

You used to check your wardrobe for signs of E.T. before going to bed each night – and were always disappointed when there was no sign of him.

You took up keyboard lessons and begged your parents for a walking piano after watching *Big*.

You remember your mates wearing so many crucifixes that it seemed like there was a massive religious revival.

The four biggest influences on your life were Maggie Thatcher and Stock, Aitken and Waterman.

You once really believed that boys found puffball skirts and pixie boots sexy.

You fantasised about a threesome with Pepsi & Shirlie and a fivesome with The Bangles.

You learned all you needed to know about self-defence from watching *The Karate Kid...*

... and all you needed to know about sex from *Just Seventeen*.

You asked your careers teacher about opportunities as a Top Gun or a Ghostbuster.

You remember parties starting with a six-pack of Double Diamond and a bottle of Liebfraumilch and ending with the contents regurgitated all over your shoes.

You found the woman
dancing in the titles of
Tales of the Unexpected
erotic (and you still do).

You wished you could own something by Sergio Tacchini, or even spell it.

You understand what's meant by a 'seven-inch single' and a 'C60 cassette'.

Your dream car at the time was an XR3i Cabriolet and your dream job was lead guitarist in Bon Jovi.

You wished your dad was
Jan-Michael Vincent from
Airwolf, your mum was
Anneka Rice and
your girlfriend was
Debbie Gibson.

You used to recite entire episodes of *The Young Ones* at the back of the chemistry lab.

Your collection of mint
condition *Transformers*
toys is worth far
more now than your
endowment mortgage.

The name 'George Michael' makes you think of 'Careless Whisper' rather than careless driving.

Your role models were Gordon Gekko, Donald Trump and Tucker from _Grange Hill_.

'Video nasties' were big news – though nowadays they're something you can watch most nights of the week on Five.

Your motto then was 'Girls Just Wanna Have Fun'. Now you'd just like a bit of peace and quiet while you listen to *The Archers*.

You'd never heard of global warming or CFCs and what's more, you didn't give a toss as long as your hair was rock solid when you went clubbing.

Partying like it was 1999
once seemed an
eternity away.

You can remember when drinking coffee wasn't particularly cool, and there were only two types to choose from: black and white.

You wanted to marry Michael J. Fox because, at the time, he was the same height as you.

You used to say, 'By the power of Grayskull, I am He-Man!' – and believe it might work.

Your first personal music
player was about four
times the size of
this book.

The Care Bears and the Smurfs were on your Christmas list (and not because you were being ironic).

Jennifer Beals in *Flashdance* was the most erotic thing you'd ever seen, until you discovered that a man did some of her dancing in the film.

You would rather go barefoot or stomp around in cereal boxes than wear the trainers your mum bought from British Home Stores.

You remember actually
laughing at Timmy Mallet,
Hale and Pace and
Ben Elton.

You had more bleach in your jeans and your hair than Kim Wilde and Billy Idol combined.

You thought the most knowledgeable authorities on pop music were Bruno Brookes, Jakki Brambles and Peter Powell.

Your make-up bag contained an almost limitless supply of electric-blue eye shadow and neon lipstick.

Miss World was essential viewing – and fun for all the family!

You once marvelled at the incredible graphics on *Thro' the Wall* on your Sinclair ZX Spectrum – they couldn't possibly get more sophisticated than that, could they?

You can trace your coming of age to the exact moment when the girls in Bucks Fizz whipped off their skirts.

You remember when there were movies that weren't based on old TV series.

You bought a Norwegian phrasebook on the off chance that you might bump into Morten Harket when you were down the shops.

You slapped your sister after arguing who was better looking in *CHiPs*: Ponch or Jon.

You used Tipp-Ex (and immediately wished you hadn't) to make stripes on your face, just like Adam Ant.

Your mum let you stay up late just so you could watch the X-rated version of the 'Thriller' video.

All the new trends – skinny jeans, Day-Glo colours and giant headphones – give you a distinct feeling of déjà vu.

You remember when *American Gigolo* was raunchy… and *Porky's* was funny.

You didn't care who shot JR and you remember wishing someone would murder Roland Rat, but you did have a soft spot for Gordon the Gopher.

You got your first grope at the school disco while snogging to Spandau Ballet's 'True'.

You remember buying
*Now That's What I Call
Music 1.*

You can sing the chorus to 'Physical' by Olivia Newton-John.

You owned a T-shirt that featured Toto's tour dates on the back... or a large smiley face on the front.

You had a mullet to rival those sported by DJ Pat Sharp and singers Paul King and Limahl.

Your perfume of choice was Poison or Giorgio Beverly Hills, and people knew you were coming twenty minutes away.

You remember all the names of Five Star. (OK, they were Stedman, Lorraine, Delroy, Denise and Doris.)

You bitterly recall being made to feel a social pariah because you had a Betamax VCR.

You remember exactly where you were when you heard that Kajagoogoo had split up.

No matter what people say, a part of you still believes that a thin leather tie with a piano keyboard printed on it looks cool.

You remember having to get up off the sofa to change channels – even though you only had four to choose from and your parents didn't let you watch radical Channel 4 anyway.

Your idea of
sophistication was
chicken Kiev accompanied
by a glass of Piat d'Or.

You were off school
for two weeks after
dislocating your shoulder
while breakdancing.

Your social life used to centre around Trivial Pursuit and Pictionary – or Twister, if your parents were cool.

Even today you wish your
company Vauxhall Vectra
could talk just like KITT
from *Knight Rider*.

Your first introduction to foreign cuisine was a Vesta dehydrated chop suey.

You're now desperately trying to get *Footloose*, *St Elmo's Fire* and *War Games* on DVD.

You were sent to your room for dancing on the bonnet of your dad's Mini Metro à la *Fame*.

Thanks to *Desperately Seeking Susan* you still have to fight the urge to dry your armpits with a hand dryer.

You once scored top marks in the *Look-in* 'How Well Do You Know Shakin' Stevens?' quiz.

You were savvy enough to know that Frankie Knuckles was a Chicago house DJ and not an associate of the Krays.

You believed the hype
about Sigue Sigue Sputnik.

You aspired to have the muscles of B. A. Baracus, but secretly fancied yourself as the new Face.

You still save the Viennetta
and Arctic Roll for your
most revered guests.

You secretly still hope that 2015 will turn out the way it is in *Back to the Future II*.

You often find yourself muttering, 'This time next year, we'll be millionaires!'

You thought your dad was the bee's knees when he pulled out a brick-sized phone at your school sports day – your mates were talking about it for weeks afterwards!

A big thank-you to the following: Philippa Hatton-Lepine; Debbie, Polly and Barney Leigh; Andrea Hatton; Martin Wheat; Liz Kershaw; Kerry Parker, and Fran Connop (a true child of the 80s).

Mark Leigh

Born in 1965, Mark spent most of his formative years in the 1980s and admits to still possessing designer stubble, a pair of stonewashed jeans and two Nik Kershaw albums. Mark's biggest regret is not having a snog at the college disco with Daisy Duke, Nena or that girl from Roxette. He is currently building a time machine.

Mike Lepine

Mike spent the 1980s being baffled at all the criticism hurled at Maggie Thatcher, since it was patently obvious to him that everyone had loads of money and was having a good time. Living in Cameron's Big Society has only made him more determined to see Maggie back in power, no matter how gaga she is now.

You Know You're a Child of the 50s When...

Helen Lincoln

ISBN: 978-1-84953-160-3

£4.99

Hardback

You Know You're a Child of the 60s When...

Mark Leigh and Mike Lepine

ISBN: 978-1-84953-161-0

£4.99

Hardback

You Know You're a Child of the 70s When...

Mark Leigh and Mike Lepine

ISBN: 978-1-84953-162-7

£4.99

Hardback

You Know You're a Child of the 90s When...

Helen Lincoln

ISBN: 978-1-84953-164-1

£4.99

Hardback

www.summersdale.com